MARRIED WITH BROKEN PIECES

AUTHOR
LaKiesha S. Thomas

Reach The Press Publishing
608 McConnell Court
Baltimore, Maryland 21220

Printed in the United States of America

Thank You

I want to Give All Praise & Honor to Jesus
Christ My Heavenly Father who is the head of
my life for allowing us to share our story of
healing and revitalization, we hope that this read
brings clarity, healing, hope, and restoration to
not just marriages but to women and men
individually as well in identifying and allowing
our God to mend their broken pieces so that they
can live their life well in Love, Joy, Peace, and
Happiness!

Thank You

To My Husband Robert Thomas Sr. I love you
dearly for being transparent to let women and
men know not only that God can change a man
but that as a man, you can choose to allow God
to guide you to be better in that change breaking
generational curses of their past. I thank you for
always being the best Dad that you know how to
be and still loving the kids and me
unconditionally and always seeking to do the
best in loving and protecting us. ***Til Death Do
Us Part I Love You!***

Thank God for our ***4 beautiful Children Robert
Jr, Ronnie, Rhea, and Royal***, God gave you to
us as your guide to life, I pray that we didn't
mess it up too much lol but that we gave you
enough to let you know with God all things are
possible, You Are Great & Special in our eyes
and the sight of God, and you can see and do
anything that your heart desires as long as you
seek God and work Hard! Love You All Dearly!

Thank You

To My Mother Carolyn Ayers, I Thank God for
you every day that you chose to always be vocal
in letting us know that we were Beautiful, Great,
Special, and that we could see and have anything
life has to offer and that with God All Things
Are Possible! You were always transparent
about your mistakes and what you believe you
could have done differently as a wife and
mother. I thank you for never speaking ill will
against our father no matter what you went
through with him, you allowed us to know and
attempt to have a relationship with him on our
own. I am so ever grateful that God chose you as
my mother; he couldn't have made a better
choice for me!

Thank You

To My Dad, Jerry London Although we didn't get to have the Father-Daughter relationship that I would have loved I thank you for being a part of giving me life and I don't know how many of your broken pieces were passed on to me, but I pray that they end with me, but I am glad that I get to share them with others to help them in healing their broken pieces. I may never know why God chose you as my father, but I know that I have and will always love you! May you continue to rest in peace, and I pray I get to see you again one day!

Thank You

To My Siblings & their mates Cedric & Quiana Wingard, Marques & La'Shone Anderson, and Allen & Shenelle Tillman I Love You Guys with all my heart I Thank God that we have one another to be an example and encouragement for one another to continue in breaking so many generational curses with one of the most significant being Marriage. I pray God gives each of us continued strength that we may be able to continually hold one another up to be a continued example to our kids and the world, letting them know that marriage is still alive, and it does work!! Love You All!

Thank You

To Uncle D & Auntie Karen, who I call my angels I don't know what I would have done if I didn't have you guys during our dark times you guys just don't know how much you mean to me. I don't know If I was getting on your nerves or wearing on you guys and if I did you never showed any frustration or aggravation you just were there whenever I called I Love You Guys Dearly, and if anyone is in need I pray that God sends them a couple like you and I pray that everything that you gave to me God has given you double! Love You Guys to Life!

Thank You

To everyone who reads this story, I pray that it causes you to take time to not reflect only on your marriage but on you as a person. Looking inside and identifying your broken pieces and asking God to help you mend them or throw them in the trash whatever it is you need to do to be healed and whole to have better relationships, friendships, and a better life. Be sure you are not pointing the finger and not pointing it back at you to see if you are not a part of the problem as well, to see if you are as forgiving as you are asking someone else to be.

Preface

A little girl born and raised in New Orleans, Louisiana grew up with 3 siblings by a single mother who told her that she could be anything she wanted to be, reminded her as often as a mom could that her little girl was beautiful, to be comfortable in her skin and that she deserves every good thing that life has to offer. Although she heard the inspirations of her mother, however, the struggle of not understanding why she still had a small space in her heart where she felt that she wasn't good enough due to her not feeling the love she desired from her father.

She almost lost what her mother taught her because of what she felt her father did not give her!

The beginning of her broken pieces

Introduction

Family is one of the most intricate parts of how we grow, learn, and carry out life around us. It creates an atmosphere of our morals, values, and how we may treat or respect others outside of the family. It's the building of self-respect, self-confidence, and self-worth. We see it all done first with family.

Love, support, forgiveness, the teaching of

our mothers, and the discipline of our

fathers of which we carry those teachings

out to the world and within our building of

a family. The bloodline of a family is

carried on from generation to generation

be it good or bad, it's when that one comes

to realize that just because it has always

been done a certain way doesn't make it

right, and there needs to be a change to

better

carry out the bloodline that has been assigned to you, changing the course for the generations to come. Will you be the one who comes forward to break the generational curses of the past bringing the change to the future generation to come which your seed will be a part of and the time starts now, call forth and cast down everything you may know to be a destructive part of your families bloodline before they are in the womb and if they are here do it now because their future depends on it and don't ignore the smallest things because the little things can slowly enlarge into something fierce causing the fight to be more enormous. The word of God has given us guidelines as to how we as a family should operate in obedience, love, forgiveness, discipline, husband & wife, mother, father and how all of these elements should be applied to have family ordered by the Lord so there won't be room for corruption. Not that we won't have troubles, but we would limit our sufferings of the present and the future.

The family should be a haven that provides love, comfort, and support, a place where you can come to receive instruction and understanding. I believe sometimes we take the gift of family and its importance for granted causing us to poorly carry out our duties as part of our family. We must be wise with whom and how we create our families.

Many of us have contended with a situation or circumstance that has made us feel left out, unwanted, forgotten, or just downright alone.

But the thing is we must decide whether or not we are going to continually use our hurt, resistant love, and attention as an excuse not to live a better life. I am not saying to just get over it but find a way to release it so that you can move forward to be the best you and have a better future. That may mean living without an answer, apology, or clarity. Remember you are not doing it for them but you.

Psalm *127:3-5 Behold, children are a heritage of the Lord: and the fruit of the womb is his reward.*

Ephesians *6:4*
4 Fathers do not provoke your children to anger but bring them up in the discipline and instruction of the Lord.

Titus 23:5
3 Likewise, teach the older women to be reverent in the way they live, not to be slanderers or addicted too much wine, but to demonstrate what is right. 4 Then they can urge the younger women to love their husbands and children, 5 to be self-controlled and pure, to be busy at home, to be kind, and to be subject to their husbands, so that no one will malign the word of God.

Married with Broken Pieces

Have you ever broken your favorite glass, mug, or vase and saw that with a little bit of glue, it could be repaired where no one ever knew it was broken? Or maybe it was broken to where you said it could be fixed with a little glue, but is it worth it. Perhaps it was broken beyond repair, so you just swept it up and threw it in the trash. Have you ever purchased an item, get home to use it and find out it is broken or missing a couple of pieces and you haven't had a chance to use it hoping you kept the receipt to bring it back to exchange it and get a new working one.

Broken or missing pieces is the state that so many marriages are in or begin causing what is to be a relationship-building of one another to be unstable from the beginning. The part that many of us have not figured out or noticed is that the broken pieces are not so much from the marriage itself but the broken pieces of each individual in the union. We are just like the broken mug, glass or vase, broken and need to be repaired knowing that with God as the glue I can be better, some feel they are broken beyond repair because of what was done to them, and some have been broken swept up the pieces, threw them in the trash but are still carrying that trash bag. Maybe you are the two who entered into a union of individual brokenness just like purchasing that item that you didn't realize some of the pieces were broken or missing until after you were married, now you're looking for the receipt (divorce), but the acknowledgment for those broken pieces is not as simple as the one at the store. The arrival of divorce bares more broken pieces to be repaired. *(Marriage becoming a shattered dream)*

My husband and I individually carried broken pieces, I had Daddy Issues and my Husband's

Mother and Father issues. We both struggled

with insecurity issues due to feeling neglected,

unwanted, or feeling we were not enough, which

if you understand the spirit of rejection or

neglect, embodies fear, seeking attention, low

self-esteem or self-worth, and a host of other

unwanted struggles for one to be challenged

with.

So many of us get married, believing that our

other half will be able to mend the broken pieces

that were broken or shattered by others.

After carrying those broken pieces for so long, the strength to find a way to repair them seems to become so challenging (*if you know me personally you know my Motto nothing is hard it's only a challenge*) it's a place where you have to dig deep, seek prayer, counseling, and work at it every day asking God to give you the guidance to mend those broken pieces. But the longer you ignore them, push them aside, you sweep them up, put them in the bag and continue to carry them as if they are a part of you the longer you hold them, they will control you.

What are the broken pieces that you need to let go of where you are saying God I am broken, and no one can put me back together but you? Are your broken pieces caused by Mother and Father Issues like my husband and I, Divorce, Abuse, Rejection, Drugs, Alcohol, or Sexual Abuse this is your time to say no more I am no longer going to allow the way someone intentionally or unintentionally shattered me have control? I will let God be the glue to mend my broken pieces.

Some of our broken pieces were passed down by our parents because their broken pieces were never repaired they either knew they were broken and ignored seeking to be restored or they had no idea or didn't understand the stance of their brokenness, you may say how wouldn't they know, I know for me I knew I wanted to be closer to my Dad but I didn't understand how much of me not having a close relationship with him would cause me to allow and accept a lot of things that I didn't deserve or how deeply broken not having that relationship had me, as you will see later on.

Your mates are not your parents and cannot restore or bring healing to the areas that you feel that you did not get from your mother or father. They can only be who they are and bring you what they have. The problem begins because so many of us get married before we have addressed and healed from our youth or past relationships bringing all of that to the table of our new relationships, making your mate suffer at the expense of the one who caused the pain. Don't blame them and run them away, they didn't do it so they shouldn't have to pay the price for it causing them you to be in a cycle of bad relationships pilling on hurt after hurt having you to feel like it's never-ending or that you don't deserve better. The process of healing is so detrimental to who you meet, I believe sometimes our spirit discerns and connects to those things of which we have suffered or presently experiencing, and we may find our self-thinking that it is for us when it is only a recognition of what you are familiar with, and we have to be careful to not confuse it with what God has for us, stay in prayer to be sure the one you are committing to is God sent.

Two Became One

Two spirits battered and bruised in need of

repair meet, with no idea of how big the bruises

on their heart were, are preparing to intertwine

the two worlds that bring love, infidelity, broken

trust with an ending of restoration of love &

peace. As a child, you sometimes don't

understand how in pieces you are until you reach

a pivotal point of adulthood and you move in

such a way that you have no answers to why you

do what you do or move the way you move until

you sit and have a quiet conversation with

yourself and God at which time he begins to

reveal how the relationships or actions of others have wounded you and they have intercepted how you should take your path in life. Now the thing is, although the actions of others have persuaded how you live your life, you have the power and choice as to how long they will have control. My mother always told me that people only do what you allow them to, so what are you going to do.

"One Whole Woman is attracted to One Whole Man.
A Half of Women is attracted to a Half of Man

1992 School Days

The bell rings, students, having loud conversations in the hallway, banging lockers as they are changing classes as I enter a new classroom, excited to see a good friend sitting across the room. I began to engage in conversation as I began to feel the stare of someone over my shoulder, turning slowly I make eye contact with the smile of a young man who I blatantly ignore with no response, with no thought to him being the future father of my children and husband. But if you know how the enemy works, he knew just what I needed *(not really)*. This would happen almost every day for a couple of weeks before I guess he decided it was the right time to finally ask me for my number after several words of flattery during the times past of which was cute, but I was close to another guy at that time, and I guess I was loyal whatever that meant at 15. But one day as we just so happen to meet leaving the library he asked for my number, still with no thought to entertain or be involved, really didn't expect him to call but he did. He wasn't a bad looking guy, but for some reason, I wasn't feeling him until we started to have some of the most entertaining conversations (don't ask me what about I have no idea lol) I just remember that we always had something to talk about and we laughed a lot, we asked one another what we wanted to know, and as time passed yes, I was falling in love "really"? So that put a damper on the relationship with the other guy, and our story begins September 12, 1992.

"She began to feel as if the hole in her heart was beginning to be filled, but to find out that it was going to be pulled further apart."

We began dating, and it was fun spending time with Robert, and we hung out a lot, and that may have been part of the problem, for one reason I didn't do as my mother said and that was if he liked me to let him pursue me *(when a man findeth a wife)* no we didn't know we were getting married at the time, but that is the base for that scripture that a man should find a woman we shouldn't find him, for there is purpose in the way the scripture was written. I always found myself going to see him. He never really tried to come over and see me, the pursuit of your happiness should be a give and take not one-sided in any relationship.

Now we are in high school, and the ups and downs of the relationship were nothing I would imagine being 16 and 17 years old, but for some reason, I just would not let it go. I would break up with him, and he would find a way to talk me into believing it would be different, he cared about me and wanted to be with me, and I would fall for it every time. So we dated through the summer, my last year of high school into college when we seem to be getting more serious for about three years.

Hanging out with the crew Charkell, Carla and Makiesha one day they would tell me I was eating more, I was always tired and would keep asking me was I pregnant I was like you all are tripping, no I'm not pregnant, well why shouldn't I be, I was not on any birth control although my mother asked if she needed to bring me a long time ago and I denied needing to do so. Robert would ask me the same, and I would have the same answer for him as well. Then I began to realize that I was starting to be more tired than usual and thought, wow, maybe I am and need to go and get checked out.

Lord how am I going to tell my mom this, I was out of high school, in college, working and probably thought I was grown but taking care of a baby I didn't know if I am ready for that, which it didn't matter if I was ready or not I was going to be someone's mother. Here comes our firstborn, a handsome baby boy Robert Jr., the love of my life I believe I wrapped a lot of my hurt up in him, dragging him back and forth, never wanting to get out just him and me.

1996 Wedding Bells

As many of us heard before my life was changed forever, I found out I was pregnant of which I was a little worried, but he was excited, had to withdraw from school at Southern University due to the pregnancy, became Mrs. Thomas as well as officially became a mother before the new year. Yep, my guy proposed after we found out that I was pregnant, although I believe it may have been a little coercion by family, feeling as though that was the right thing to do, and I said no. Yes, I said no, I was going to have to tell my mother who told me from the beginning he was not the guy for me, and she knew I was pregnant before I could even tell her *"The holy spirit knows all.;.* You see Robert, and I had this roller-coaster relationship, girls harassing me about him, finding pictures of other girls with notes attached, just a mess, all the signs were there, but I was trying to fill that void. You see you do what you learn though, I love my father dearly and miss him momentously may he rest in peace but I feel all of my life I had to chase for my father's affection. We never had the relationship where he came and took me out for ice cream or call me princess or any of the things, I see my husband do with our daughter.

If I wanted to see him or spend time with my Dad, I had to initiate it, which I believe I carried into the relationship with my husband. I chased him throughout the dating relationship good, bad, and ugly. See, that's why the involvement of both parents is so pivotal in the lives of their children because all the things I wanted to hear from my father, my mother shared those words of love and inspiration with myself and my siblings. She always told us we were beautiful, and that if a man wants to be with you let him pursue you, and we could do anything that we set our minds to, we were her little princesses and prince. For some reason, none of that could feel that void of wanting to be wanted by my father.

September 21, 1996, Robert and I had the best wedding ever to say our families put it together in about two weeks. It was a party. I finally said yes and built up the courage to tell my mom after a couple of months, and our families made sure we had a good time; it wasn't the most lavish or expensive, but it was beautiful, and I was officially Mrs. Thomas. Oh, how short that lovely time would end. I believe my firstborn was about 4 or 5 months, and I received a call from the other woman who made it her business to let me know I wasn't the one he wanted, although I was the one he gave his last name. As I talked about before, I believe he was coerced, I thought he cared about me but marry me wasn't too sure about that especially after all the headaches I'd experienced during the first three years we were together. The question is, why would you marry him if you had any doubt? Not wanting to be a single parent, he was my first, especially growing up in a saved (Christian) family, I was already being whispered about when it was said that I was pregnant, I know better right. I was a little disappointed in myself as well, but being saved or knowing Christ doesn't exempt you from being broken and not knowing how to process your brokenness as well as maturely walk in the gifts of the spirit to be free from it at 20. You know at that age you think you know everything just because you have a job, car a few dollars in your pocket while getting a degree but know nothing. So, all though I was fully operating in all the characteristics of being an adult, learning how to live a Christian life, I still had a lot to learn about myself and life experiences, all while doing it as a broken wife and mother.

"The Catastrophes of being broken and unequally yoked

1999 A Dream Short-Lived

Yes! I finally graduated with a degree in Criminal Justice and now ready to pursue either a master's degree or law school, which never happened. Robert presents a move to the ATL. In excitement, I agree, because I always talked about living outside the city of New Orleans, not that I didn't love home. I just wanted to experience life somewhere different for a while. I thought ok, this may bring some change, our marriage wasn't at its worst yet, but it wasn't the best either. He was pursuing a rap career, which consisted of late nights, clubs that weren't so much of my preference and that I couldn't attend

being that we had a son that needed to be cared

for. So here we are in Atlanta about to start this

new life, which lasted all about three months,

and we were back in New Orleans. The whole

time we were there it wasn't too much different,

he was either working of which we both were, at

the studio or driving back and forth to New

Orleans which I believe to see the other woman,

yes, the woman who decided to call me right

after we were married, that had been a thorn in

my side since that day, *"remember the chase."*

He also found another young lady to entertain while we were in Atlanta as well. So here we are back in New Orleans with no place to live because the money we had to move to Atlanta was gone, and we weren't there long enough to save any money to relocate back and get our place, so we moved in with his family.

2001 At Wit's end Or Not?

Returning from Atlanta, I was frustrated and felt like lord what to do, but you know I'm trying to work it outright; it's the good days that give you hope that things will turn for the better. After staying with his family for 2 1/2years and continually having the arguments about moving into our place, continued discussions about other women, late nights out no phone calls, until one day, he says I'm not in love with you anymore.

It's one thing to feel that way, but for him to say
it straight to your face, makes every part of how
you think about you and that relationship
crumble in a way you can't imagine. Thank the
Lord my mother taught us how to save, I was
able to move into my place with myself and my
son. As I was preparing to move, I received a job
that I had been waiting on to call that paid more
money than my current employer at that time
(God is a keeper). It was unnerving at first
because although our relationship wasn't the
best, he was there, and now I was all alone.

What made it even lonelier was all my siblings and my mother, who all were my safety net, were gone. They had all moved away. Thank God he had a Ram in the bush to keep me together and focus when I thought I would lose it at times, my good friend Karen and her Husband Uncle D who was my husband's uncle, till this day I thank God for them, sometimes I felt like they were my angels. Now I sat sometimes and said to myself, is this over? I would say if so, do I care if it is. The truth of the matter was I did care but had to come to grips with it may just be over or maybe not.

After living alone for about two months, yep, he moved in, crazy right, no, he was my husband and knew how to say what I needed to hear *(or wanted to hear)* to make me feel everything was going to be different. We never stopped talking to one another from the time I left, he would drop me off and pick me up from work and come by when he got off from work. My mother would always remind me that I didn't have to put up with it, and it was up to me to demand change for me and that I knew how much I could tolerate, that I had to realize that I didn't deserve mistreatment.

But for some reason, again I just couldn't let go or didn't want to let go, just like I didn't want to give up hope of having a real bonding relationship with my father.

Ephesians 5:25 For Husbands, this means love your wives, just as Christ loved the church, he gave up his life for her

Not long after he moved in, it was back to the same chaos as before, no calls, no show, arguments and before I knew it, I was in tears on the phone telling my sister that I am pregnant again, that was the last thing we needed in the state our relationship was in.

I guess the stress of our relationship was causing me to have horrible pain early in the pregnancy to where I was in such discomfort at work the doctor suggested bed rest, so I refused to allow him to stress me the entire pregnancy so off to Maryland I went by my mother. He would call us day in and day out checking on us asking if we needed anything, he hopes I come back after the baby comes, it was exhausting even being away, but I was able to control it better because he couldn't just show up at my doorstep if I had enough for the week I could just ignore his calls or just let our oldest talk to him and be done because one thing for sure he was and has always been there as a dad. I remember one day

driving home from a doctors appt I was crying

and arguing with God complaining about why I

have to be way out here and going through this

pregnancy all by myself, and he is out there in

New Orleans having fun doing whatever he

wants to do just fussing and complaining driving

on the way back to my mom's house. Then that

night I remember sitting up watching Juanita

Bynum on TBN, and the phone rang it was late

like midnight I thought it was my husband

calling that late, but it was my sister Trell in

Germany, it was almost like she was in the car

with me earlier on that ride home.

When I picked up the phone she was praying in her heavenly language, and she spoke a word from the Lord that made me just cry myself to sleep thanking the Lord for hearing me, she said the Lord said that my husband was not my source or my provider, he is, see I was seeking for my husband to fill a place in my life that he couldn't only God could do that and until I was willing to allow God to do that I would continue to accept all the mishaps that my husband continued to bring in our lives.

Time for baby to arrive which was our second

oldest Ronnie, he comes up to Maryland, travels

back to New Orleans, and prepares for us to

return with the agreement that we are going to

work it out, and he would have us a place of our

own. Although every part of me was saying no, I

hopped on the train with my two little people,

and back to New Orleans, we went. As we exit

the train, our oldest in excitement runs to

embrace him, and as we approach one another,

we embraced which felt nothing like he

belonged to me, but he delivered our place to

live had it prepared just as he said.

I was able to obtain my old job back, and we were a family for once for about six months. And who I get a call from again, by this time I am passed tired, the ups, downs, late nights, early mornings it's all just enough. I'm mad with myself because I knew not to come back. One day I checked his messages and hear a voice message from the other women saying she was waiting for them to get married, I was like she must know something I don't know because he never says anything about divorce to me, but who knows what was being told to her just like all the lies that were being expressed to me.

He came in one morning, from the day before with donuts for the kids, no apology nothing, another time he went to Dallas for a show and took her while I was at home with our kids. The final straw was when he came home as we were sleeping one-night yelling get up, I could smell the liquor before he came closer asking me to leave and leave the kids, I knew he had been with her. I called his Uncle to ask him to talk to him, being his Uncle knew my Dad was an Officer he suggested that I call him. My dad and one of his officer friends came over, arguments flaring until it became silent, and my dad was sure I was ok.

He began apologizing, professing his love, and I laid down with the thought ok this is over.

One day while he was at work my dad helped me move my things out over to his house, I didn't want to allow him to talk me out of leaving, I wanted to be done with him. I felt like this can't be life, and it wasn't going to be suitable for the kids as they became older. After I left, he was upset, and we didn't say much to one another other than partaking in the responsibility of caring for the kids.

I mean how selfish, how are you mad that I left

when you didn't act as if you wanted me there in

the first place, but after all the continuous

cheating and lies I *allowed myself* to deal with I

finally stood my ground and was like enough is

enough I am better than this and deserve more.

But my husband just would not let me be.

2004 To Be Or Not

After living with my dad for several months working and getting myself together to begin preparing myself to be divorced, he went out and found a Pastor for us to get marriage counseling, *Ha! Excellent Time to Suggest Counseling Right LOL!* I said what could be the worst that could happen after all that we had already been through, so I agreed to go.

During counseling it came up about moving back to Atlanta again because he was still pursuing music at the time, NO SIR you got me once you're not going to get me again leaving

my job and taking me out of a place of having

some help with the kids not sure if he was ready

to change. We continued with counseling, and it

was going well, *so I thought,* but after all the

sessions, we still found ourselves saying our

goodbyes and having discussions on how we

would parent the kids between New Orleans and

Atlanta and so he went.

Not long after getting my oil change, the manager at the counter, and I engaged in a friendly conversation, and we found our self-exchanging numbers. Now what state of mind I was in at the time was not stable at all because he asked me over to his home the first week I met him, Hmmmmm now we all know what that was about but guess what I went, and no one knew with who or where I was *Thank You Lord for Keeping ME!* I didn't even tell my good friend Karen who I shared a lot of things with.

Truth be told I really wanted to get back at my husband but would I have been getting back at him or hurting myself because I didn't know that man and after not going through with his sexual request the first time had the nerve to go back again and had it in my head that I was going to attempt to go through with it this time, but something came over me that made me so afraid that I just put my shoes back on and walked out the door and never went back again. He continued to call attempting to persuade me, and we still had great conversations, which was more than likely apart of the persuasion *You Think*!

I remember after meeting him I talked to my mom one day and was telling her about him *excluding the visits to his home*, my mom was like oh yeah that's fine, but you are still married, and I am like really mom you mean to tell me after all the Hell and High Water I have been through with that man that's what you are going to say, which should not have been a surprise knowing that is how it has always been living according to the word of God in our home, but later on I understood what she meant, it wasn't that she didn't care about what I had been through my mom just was being sure that she didn't agree with a situation that wasn't good for me and find myself in something worse than what I was already in. The funny thing was when Mr. found out that was I talking to someone he didn't take it so well although he tried to act as if it didn't concern him, he would call me at all hours of the night and early mornings, I'm guessing to see where I would be but a lot of times I didn't answer or gave the responses of being unbothered and busy with little time to talk to him. So, from there on, we spoke to one another less and less.

Hurricane Katrina was Enroot to hit New Orleans catastrophically and just so happen my mom was in town with my uncle doing ministry at that time, so I had some help with packing up the boys and me to evacuate. It took us maybe a little over a day to get to Maryland that's how bad the traffic was from New Orleans all the way there with a whole city of people attempting to evacuate, we had to sleep at a rest stop along the way believe it or not most of the hotels were full or charging excruciating prices, it was about three or four carloads of us traveling together it was exhausting.

During our travel, the signals weren't the best

with our cellphones, so while family members

are watching the news and started to see the

tragedy of the water coming into the city, they

began trying to contact us, and they weren't

successful, so a lot of them began to worry. My

husband was so upset because he didn't know

where we were and if we were ok and at that

time it was probably a host of emotions going on

with me, tired of our marriage, tired from

traveling for almost two days with my babies

and family so when we did arrive,

I wasn't in any urgent hurry to make an effort to

call him and let him know not me, but the kids

were all right, so again, we argued about that.

So now we are on the east coast attempting to

figure out what is our next move because now

New Orleans is not an option for the moment

and neither is us getting back together so look

like Maryland is home for now although that

wasn't my choice it was a blessing and comfort

to be with family my mom, my baby brother and

my baby sister who was just a two-hour ride in

Delaware, who we would go see often on the

weekends, my middle sister was away in

Germany. So I made the best of the time we

spent there during that time.

Till Death Do Us

The Holidays are here, and unfortunately, he asked if the kids could come and spend it with him in Atlanta, no matter how upset and frustrated I was with our relationship I never wanted to keep our kids away from him, and he was always there for them because at the end of it all they needed both of us. I didn't want to, but I said it was okay if they spent the Christmas Holidays with him, although it was going to be him and the other woman like they were one big happy family, I humbly obliged being he hadn't seen them as much since he moved there earlier that year and the whole situation with us moving to the East Coast due to Katrina. He drove from Atlanta with the other woman to get them, they spent the holiday's with them, and he drove them back, but this time he came alone, and he had the nerve to tell me we were going to get back together, I laughed and told him he was crazy, now how are you going to say that after you just spent the Christmas holidays with someone else, not to mention he was trying to get me to hug him while she was sitting in the car when they came to pick the kids up. When my husband brought the kids back to Maryland, after the holiday's he made a turnaround trip, I guess he had to make it back so she wouldn't feel some type of way knowing she let him come and bring the kids alone, but we talked just about his entire ride back.

After that, he began to call every day while he was at work, of course, not when he was home because she was there. I must be honest; it was almost like we were starting all over again, although I still didn't trust him or believed we were going to be together. So we proceeded with our daily talks about mostly us repairing our marriage of which I had to seek God on because the past played back amid those good conversations and we have been here before so why would it be different this time, but if we

were I had to be clear in my heart and thoughts,

so I wrote a prayer, and I was particular about

what I wanted from God either he was going to

help me be healed and release myself from my

husband if he wasn't serious about changing or

help me to see him in his honest place and

forgive him if he was, detailing every change I

wanted to see in our relationship, made a couple

of copies taped it up in an envelope and gave

one to my mother, grandmother and my uncle a

couple of prayer warriors and asked them to

agree with me in prayer. A few weekends later

we would travel to Delaware where my sister

and uncle lived and had family prayer, and my

uncle came out with the envelope just as I gave

it to him never opened and repeated to me what I

wrote in that prayer letter to me and said God

said it was well for me to get back with my

husband. That was my confirmation. After all, I

had never told any of my family that I was even

thinking about us getting back together because I

didn't want to set myself up for hurt and

disappointment again.

Not shortly after I remember he called me one

day and said I'm going to call you tomorrow and

tell you everything and I was a little baffled

because that was the first thing he said as soon

as I answered the phone I don't know if he went

to sleep with that on his heart or woke up with it

or both. I said ok, tell me everything about

what? He replied us, everything that I lied about

and I said ok, just as he said he would he told me

everything even some things that I had not even

a clue about and then a couple of days later I

was attempting to call him and his phone was off

for some reason I knew it had something to do

with her and my husband called me later on,

from I believe may have been a payphone and I

asked him did she turn off his phone and he told

me, yes she did, she probably noticed his call log

where we talked every day and figured she

wasn't having it.

2006

Back Together
Again

One night we were on the phone planning us

getting back together, where did we want to live

and things of that nature and a phone call came

through, and he asked me to hold on when he

came back all my husband said was I'm so sorry

for messing up our family and I am saying what

happened, but he kept repeating it, and I said

what is it.

She said that she is pregnant, complete silence came across the line for about 2 to 3 minutes I told him I would call him back as the tears began to flow, and as we hung up, he said he was sorry again. It was late, but I had to call my friend Karen and ask her what did she think because I was like is this baby going to be the demise of what I thought was going to be what God said it would be, was I going to have to deal with the baby mama drama because although I didn't have an issue with her she sure seemed to have a problem with me and I am his wife, but I knew what that was about. But Karen, initially she said o wow, and she didn't want to give me an answer because she didn't want to tell me anything

wrong, which I understood. After all, that wasn't

something she had to deal with before, and I

respected her for not giving me that girl if I was

you, answer. After all, I believe it's easy for us to

say that when we haven't experienced a situation

personally. However, we spoke a couple of days

later, and Karen told me Kiesha, if you forgive

your husband, you believe in your heart that he

is sincere, and you want to get back together do

it. Although we were married on paper, we

hadn't been together physically for two years.

That night after I hung up with Karen, I woke my mom, who was in the other room, asked her the same thing. She said if you believe your husband is sincere and you can forgive him without reminding him of everything from the past, don't let your marriage go. I slept on it and prayed and cried another day or two, but I had to remember the word that my uncle gave me about my prayer. After that, I was like ok Lord, I'm going back *((Luke 10:17-19)." Let God be true, and every man a liar. Whose report shall you believe? I shall believe the report of the Lord.*

We were back planning our reunion. We couldn't go back to New Orleans, which neither of us wanted to, so we made Houston, Texas, our home. No, everything wasn't all is well. We were still in a place of working and coming into a new home together. Although I said yes, I continued in my struggle of dealing with another child that was not my own coming into our world in the midst of trying to heal and recover, of who I wasn't or never would be mad with or treat indifferently because she had nothing to do with what her mother and father chose to do.

"Don't destroy children for adult actions"

The things that bothered me first was what would be the dynamic of this new environment that I was subjecting myself to of an outside child and her mother, you hear all these baby mama stories and all the cattiness, fighting and bickering and I did not want to have any parts of that and refused to be getting into it with someone every time it came to my husband ensuring that he is a part of his child's life. My second heartache was that she was giving my husband something I had prayed for some years, she would give him his first little girl, now what would that add to this family circle, if it didn't already feel like a slap in the face.

I had to go back into prayer and be sure that I was sure this is what I wanted to do, and with God's strength, could I handle it. We say that God is in control, but do we know that he is.

After moving forward my husband and I were coming to be in a trustworthy place, relearning one another, growing seeing things more as a couple, I was so surprisingly comfortable with my husband and how he was walking as a man of his word in all that he confessed and professed in us reuniting as well as having a miss carriage God blessed us with our first and only baby girl, which I believe in my heart gave her to us knowing what would be the attempt of the enemy to try and bring confusion back to our relationship with him having a daughter outside of the home, But God! When we pray, he will answer and fight on our behalf.

My husband and I have been back together 14 years, and I believe God is not through with us yet, there is so much more for us to see do and say to encourage, inspire and touch the lives of others, we don't have it all together and have things that we work on every day but we are better, moving forward along with God as our guide.

The way God allowed us to reconcile and move

forward may not be what God has or desires for

you and your mate. However, we are a testament

that if you wanted to work with the commitment

on both parts and God as the center of your

union, I would say it will work.

The Recovery

Recover: *To return to a healthy state of mind and strength*

After going through a tragedy or a rough time in our lives, we want to get back to what is normal, and we want it now! Asking why is this process taking so long, or why do I have to go through all of this just to get back to where I was or want to be. Those thoughts and many of our actions to rush to the recovery process is the very reason many of us find ourselves back where we didn't want to be or somewhere even worse.

The method of recovery is just that a process and you can't rush through it because if you do you may miss a valuable lesson or something won't heal properly causing it to be easily broken again with the possibility of never properly improving at all, especially if there is no guidance on how to properly go through your recovery process. If you are recovering from a traumatic illness or accident, there is a doctor to give you specific instructions on what it is you need to do to go through the most efficient and effective recovery process, now if you decide to take a short cut through those instructions there may be a need for you to go back and see the doctor and possibly a more extensive recovery.

During my husband and I separation, it was my recovery period to regain focus and come back to a healthy state of mind. You see, when my husband and I separated early on if I would have taken my time and listened to God and went through the process of him bringing me back to a clear state of mind there would not have been a need for us to go through with a separation a second time. I believe that I extended the time on our separation the second time because I chose to do what I wanted to do and not what God would have me to do.

That's how most of us end up in a *"How Did I Get Here"* situation because God was never asked or allowed to speak to our hearts the words of wisdom we needed so we go our way until it falls apart and then we run back to God to seek the knowledge we should have requested from the beginning. I remember once asking my mom why did God let me marry him, and she said God will give us the desires of our heart, I believe she meant God allowed me to marry him knowing I would have to come back to him and surely I did. The truth is that I never really sought out God on that decision because I was operating out of my broken pieces at the time, although I knew God and knew his word, I allowed my brokenness to speak to me and not God. When you are in the recovery or any major decision, you should not have any counsel, but God (someone of Godly council) too many voices, comments, opinions can cause your thoughts to be cloudy and unable to make a sound judgment. Go back to the Doctor. Scenario if the Dr. said you had to walk up and down the stairs three times a day to change the condition of your health, and then you get opinions and suggestions from a host of others who are not medical experts you may find yourself in a place of I don't know if any of this will work not even what the Dr. said allowing

the pain to speak louder than the words of the Dr

causing you to feel as if you'll never heal or heal

properly. So many of us are allowing our

brokenness to speak louder than any counsel

now in our lives, but we think we are ok because

we have happy moments, successful careers,

beautiful families, or even successful marriages.

It's almost like a "functional addict." You

believe that you are ok until you said you don't

want to do the drugs or drink the alcohol

anymore and you began to go through the

symptoms of withdrawal and realize you weren't

as strong or ok as you thought, see you needed

the substance to make it through the day and it's when you didn't have it, is when you seem to feel that everything around you isn't going the way you think it should. What part of you is broken and it has you holding on to that thing that you think if you let it go things won't go well but if you could only understand that if you allow it to go how much more beautiful life, your marriage, friendships, careers would be fulfilling, know that it's hurting you more than its helping you, you may not even realize how many decisions you have made and are making in those broken pieces especially in your marriage. We must work diligently in being free from our broken pieces so that it won't fall on and be repeated by our kids.

During our separation I spent a lot of quiet time with God, no longer dwelling on the distrust and misery I was having with my husband, I finally allowed myself to understand that I could not control him or our situation and if it was going to change it would have to be God to be the one to do it. I began to work on me, and what it was I wanted to see happen in my life for the future, what I should have been doing from the beginning. I told God, ok, I give up because I know he was probably saying "about time!" Is that you trying to control your situation on your own, only causing your frustrations to become out of control, causing yourself even more hurt, sadness, or depression? Once I gave it all over to God, I found me in so much peace that I was able to have better conversations with my husband, although we were still in the midst of us not being together and him possibly being with someone else. I had come to a place of comfort that it wasn't all about him anymore but me and God. I began to work on moving forward in pursuing the goals that I set aside for the last couple of years. I started writing my visions, researching how to start my own business, something I always dreamed of. Every day I found myself becoming more excited about what

God was going to do in my life.

Matthew 11:28
*Come to me, all who are weary and burdened,
and I will give you rest. Take my yoke upon you
and learn from me, for I am gentle and humble
in heart, and you will find rest for your souls.
For my yoke is easy and my burden is light*

Proverbs 12:25
*Anxiety weighs down the heart, but a kind word
cheers it up*

1 Peter 5:7
*Cast all your anxiety on him because he cares
for you.*

After reuniting in 2006 it was like we were never apart the butterflies that had turned into almost hate for my husband were back, now I would be lying if I said that doubt didn't try to creep in several times along this time of recovery, attempting to push the feeling of its going to be the same as before but my husband's actions continued to reassure what God had spoken to me through my uncle several months before that everything would be well.

He would hold my hand more, the embrace I felt was so different as if he missed me, I could feel the difference, to see him leave the room and not have to take his phone with him or if he was leaving the house always concerned if I was ok and if I wanted to come along even if it was just going to the store and back. Calling during lunch breaks at work regularly. Now some may say that's all, but when you were living in the shadow of someone for an extended time of someone's life who not only told you that they love you looking you in the eye and said until death do us part, that feeling is beautiful to have them live up to the life they committed to.

We have grown in our conversations and how we listen and try and understand one another's feelings. We hear one another much better now. My husband and I were like the purchase you made and didn't realize some of the pieces were missing or it was broken before you even had the chance to use it, we were broken before we ever attempted to enjoy our marriage. We were young supposed to be in love and didn't realize how many pieces were missing, from each of us individually that would be needed in living the life of marriage together. We could have brought it back (got a divorce) but I believe both of our broken pieces were pulling on one another trying

to survive, like that purchase that was missing a

screw and you went looked in the toolbox are

junk drawer to see if you had a screw that would

fit and it may have worked for a while but

because it wasn't the screw that came with it, it

began to fall apart. But GOD! He was the

missing screw that is holding us completely

together. Now we are in a continuous process of

being that glass that you broke, used a little glue

to put it back together to look as though it was

never broken.

God has mended us together that some don't

believe when we tell the testimony that we were

ever in the place that we were in. But the first

thing is to acknowledge what it is that is broken

and in marriage so many times we want to point

the finger and say it was all the other person

fault and never looking at our self and seeing

what part we played in our demise or where we

allowed our broken pieces to overtake us and

lose where we should be winning. As for me, I

was feeling like I was going to lose if I didn't

chase my husband, so I didn't go to graduate or

law school, which was something I had in my

heart to do, was that his fault no I had control

over that if I would have allowed my focus to be

on God and my babies and my goals and

allowed God to fight on my behalf I would have

achieved what I had set out to do. I frustrated

myself daily worrying about what he was doing,

where was he going, was he with her causing

myself to have all types of anxiety if I would

have just listened to the words of my mother.

Proverbs 18:22 He who finds a wife finds a good thing and

obtains favor of the Lord...

No One or nothing should have you in a place where it is sucking the life out of you, because when you do find yourself trying to fill the void of those broken pieces you fill them with things like alcohol, drugs, sex, food, shopping, social media, a man or a woman, anger that will bring more significant pain, hurt or destruction, adding to your broken pieces, let it go. Stop telling yourself you're ok and be free for real and let God fill your void and mend your broken pieces.

John 8:36
So, if the Son sets you free you will be free indeed

I believe that so many marriages have ended are headed to divorce because each individual has not taken the time to express the part they played and where they are a part of the issue in the marriage, what are the broken pieces that you have brought to the union that is causing the yoke in the marital union to be divided., I would write notes to my husband when I wanted to say something to him, what in the world is that? You are in the same house with the person you are supposed to love and spend the rest of your life with, and you can't talk to one another face to face and had no idea of why I felt that I needed to do that or why I felt that was ok until I seen my own Dad do the same thing to me while living in his home with him at the beginning of our separation. So all though he may have been involved in matters of infidelity how was I making him feel not only as a man but just as a person overall that I couldn't have a simple conversation with him face to face and for some reason or another we as women have this idea that men don't have feelings as we do or we shouldn't treat them with the same emotional respect that we desire, just like they do to one another we treat them with the same saying that they need to Man Up!

But ladies just a little note for you men want to feel needed and wanted as well. Now does that excuse him from his actions, not at all, it just lets us know that we must look at our issues just as we look at theirs.

For all my Sisters and Brothers who have decided to use your brokenness as an excuse to step outside of your marriage and play the blame game and say all the things that your mate wasn't or isn't doing as to why you chose to step out, Stop It! Especially if you have never allowed your mate to hear your concerns and even after that you still don't have the right to just go and spiritually allow someone else into the intimate part of your union. See so many of us believe we become one when we walk down the aisle or stand in front the preacher or judge at the courthouse but when we lie down together our spirits become one and when you choose to do the same with someone else you have brought them into the ties of your union. *"Soul Ties"*

The Two Shall Become One Flesh.

Mark 10:6-8
But at the beginning of creation, God made them male and female. For this reason, man shall leave his mother and father and be united to his wife, and two will become one flesh. So they are no longer two, but one flesh. Therefore what God has joined together, let no one separate.

Hebrews 13:4
Marriage is honorable in all, and the bed undefiled, but whoremongers and adulterers God will judge.

For the man or woman who has decided to step outside of the marriage and realize you don't want to lose your mate have asked for an opportunity to get it right, know that in the instance that it was brought to them that you have betrayed their trust it is an immediate matter of starting over and that is a matter of taking time to rebuild, and it will not happen overnight, you see you have to understand it is not only them trying to trust you again but in the same process trying to heal from the hurt they feel you have caused.

So if you want to work it out, you have to give

them back that comfort to trust you again doing

what it takes to provide them with the security to

know that you mean what you say by not just

saying but doing. Now for the sister or brother

who is on the side of healing and building trust

and you are saying that you want to work it out

and be together you cannot continue to beat

them over and over again with their previous

actions if they are showing you that they are

apologetic for their actions and are moving

towards doing things differently and being better

give them space and opportunity to do

that. This must be like anything else you have to both do your part to work together.

We have to take the time to pray and get to know who we are choosing to say we want to spend the rest of our life with and find ourselves in a short-lived romance of which is not totally what marriage is all about, yes there are parts of excitement to be expected. However, marriage overall is a covenant between you, your mate, and God. That is, you will allow God to be the lead to get you through the Happy, Sad, Good, Bad & Ugly of which you are more than likely to experience a little bit of it all.

Don't let your broken pieces speak for you, allowing you to connect with the familiar, which may be with the life of someone of the same broken pieces or someone whose broken pieces may almost be at a state of beyond repair. We also must remember that those broken pieces may carry generational curses that all will be a part of the union you have come in covenant with as well as passed on to your kids. Take time to heal before you move on to another relationship so that you won't bleed on those who did not create your broken pieces making them pay for what they had no part in creating.

Matters of the Heart
Words to Live By

A Woman was derived from the ribs of Man and Man is birth (given life) through a woman in continuing the cycle of human life. We should love and appreciate one another just as God has created us. Even in all of our faults, we need one another in the strengths we were given to help one another progress and move forward in this life. Brothers love the women as Christ loves the church, and Sisters lets support and respect our men so that we can be the example that our children need.

Ecclesiastes 4:12:

"Though one may be overpowered, two can defend themselves. A cord of three strands is not quickly broken."

1 Peter 3:7:

"In the same way, you husbands must give honor to your wives. Treat your wife with understanding as you live together. She may be weaker than you are, but she is your equal partner in God's gift of new life. Treat her as you should so your prayers will not be hindered."

Ephesians 5:25-33

"Husbands, love your wives, as Christ loved the church and gave himself up for her, that he might sanctify her, having cleansed her by the washing of water with the word, so that he might present the church to himself in splendor, without spot or wrinkle or any such thing, that she might be holy and without blemish. In the same way, husbands should love their wives as their own bodies. He who loves his wife loves himself. For no one ever hated his own flesh, but nourishes and cherishes it, just as Christ does the church,"

Proverbs 31:11-12

"The heart of her husband doth safely trust in her so that he shall not need spoil. She will do him good and not evil all the days of her life."

Colossians 3:18

"Wives, submit yourselves unto your own husbands, as it is fit in the Lord."

Proverbs 31:10-12

An excellent wife, who can find? For her worth is far above jewels. The heart of her husband trusts in her, and he will have no lack of gain. She does him good and not evil all the days of her life.

1 Peter 3: 3-4

Your beauty should not consist of outward things like elaborate hairstyles and the wearing of gold ornaments or beautiful clothes. Instead, it should consist of what is inside the heart with the imperishable quality of a gentle and quiet spirit, which is very valuable in God's eyes.

Genesis 2:24

That is why a man leaves his father and mother and is united to his wife, and they become one flesh.

Proverbs 31:10-30

10 A wife of noble character who can find? She is worth far more than rubies.

11 Her husband has full confidence in her and lacks nothing of value.

12 She brings him good, not harm, all the days of her life.

13 She selects wool and flax and works with eager hands.

14 She is like the merchant ships, bringing her food from afar.

15 She gets up while it is still night; she provides food for her family and portions for her female servants.

16 She considers a field and buys it; out of her earnings, she plants a vineyard.

17 She sets about her work vigorously; her arms are strong for her tasks.

18 She sees that her trading is profitable, and her lamp does not go out at night.

19 In her hand, she holds the distaff and grasps the spindle with her fingers.

20 She opens her arms to the poor and extends her hands to the needy.

21 When it snows, she has no fear for her household; for all of them are clothed in scarlet.

22 She makes coverings for her bed; she is clothed in fine linen and purple.

23 Her husband is respected at the city gate, where he takes his seat among the elders of the land.

24 She makes linen garments and sells them, and supplies the merchants with sashes.

25 She is clothed with strength and dignity; she can laugh at the days to come.

26 She speaks with wisdom, and faithful instruction is on her tongue.

27 She watches over the affairs of her household and does not eat the bread of idleness.

28 Her children arise and call her blessed; her husband also, and he praises her:

29 "Many women do noble things, but you surpass them all."

30 Charm is deceptive, and beauty is fleeting, but a woman

who fears the LORD is to be praised

Made in the USA
Coppell, TX
25 August 2022

82036313R00069